Reading
a Map

by Emma Huddleston

FOCUS
READERS®

PIONEER

www.focusreaders.com

Focus Readers is distributed by North Star Editions:
sales@northstareditions.com | 888-417-0195

Produced for Focus Readers by Red Line Editorial.

Photographs ©: Shutterstock Images, cover, 1, 8, 12, 21; iStockphoto, 4, 7, 15, 16, 19; Red Line Editorial, 11

Library of Congress Cataloging-in-Publication Data
Names: Huddleston, Emma, author.
Title: Reading a map / [by Emma Huddleston].
Description: Lake Elmo, Minnesota : Focus Readers, [2021] | Series: Life
   skills | Includes index. | Audience: Grades 2-3
Identifiers: LCCN 2020002246 (print) | LCCN 2020002247 (ebook) | ISBN
   9781644933466 (Hardcover) | ISBN 9781644934227 (Paperback) | ISBN
   9781644935743 (PDF) | ISBN 9781644934982 (eBook)
Subjects: LCSH: Map reading--Juvenile literature. | Maps--Juvenile
   literature. | Cartographic materials--Juvenile literature.
Classification: LCC GA130 .H84 2021 (print) | LCC GA130 (ebook) | DDC
   912.01/4--dc23
LC record available at https://lccn.loc.gov/2020002246
LC ebook record available at https://lccn.loc.gov/2020002247

Printed in the United States of America
Mankato, MN
082020

About the Author

Emma Huddleston lives in the Twin Cities with her husband. She enjoys reading, writing, and swing dancing. She uses maps every day to avoid getting lost.

Table of Contents

Chapter 1

Helpful Maps

A map is an **overhead** drawing of a place. People read maps to find **directions**. Maps also help people learn about places.

Maps can show large or small areas. Large areas include countries or states. Small areas include cities or parks. Lines show borders. A border separates one area from another.

Fun Fact

A map of a park might show details such as buildings or paths.

Chapter 2

Title and Key

First, look at the map's **title**. The title tells what you are looking at. Other words on the map tell the names of places.

Next, look at the **key**. It tells you how to read the map. It shows what **symbols** or colors mean. Stars or large dots often mark big cities. Green often stands for parks. Blue usually stands for water.

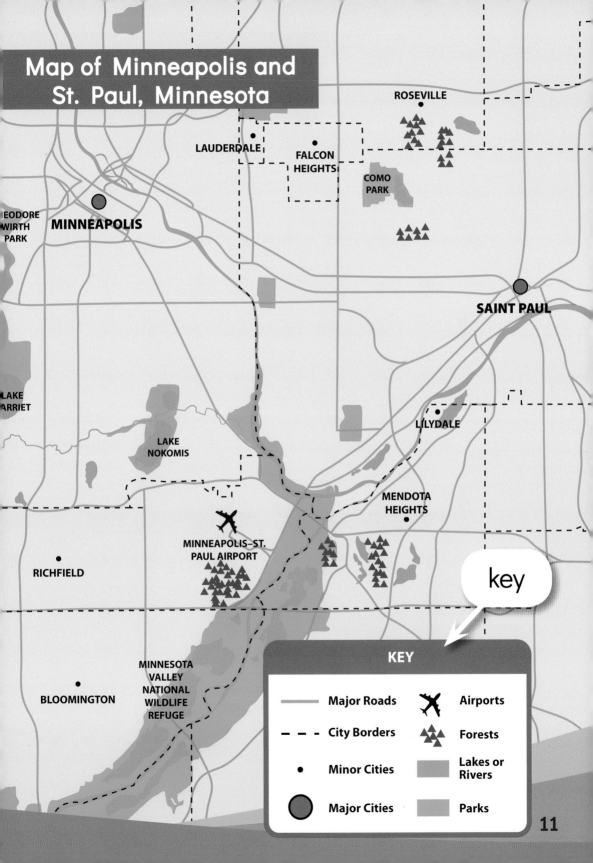

Map of Minneapolis and St. Paul, Minnesota

ROSEVILLE

LAUDERDALE

FALCON HEIGHTS

COMO PARK

EODORE WIRTH PARK

MINNEAPOLIS

LAKE HARRIET

LAKE NOKOMIS

SAINT PAUL

LILYDALE

MENDOTA HEIGHTS

MINNEAPOLIS–ST. PAUL AIRPORT

RICHFIELD

key

MINNESOTA VALLEY NATIONAL WILDLIFE REFUGE

BLOOMINGTON

KEY

Major Roads		Airports	
City Borders		Forests	
Minor Cities		Lakes or Rivers	
Major Cities		Parks	

Chapter 3

Other Details

Look at the **compass rose** next. This symbol shows which way is north, south, east, and west.

Then, look at the **scale**. Maps are smaller than the places they show. The scale shows how far apart areas are from one another in real life. For example, 100 miles (160 km) in real life might be just 1 inch (2.5 cm) on the map.

STANDARD TIME

Carlsbad Caverns
32 Nat'l Park

Lamesa

Hobbs
Carlsbad

Snyder

Sweetwater

Midland

Fort Worth

El Paso

Ciudad Juárez
Pecos

Odessa

Big Spring

Abilene

Corsic

Fort Stockton

San Angelo

Pecos

T   E   X   A   S.

Brownwood Waco

Te

Alpine

Big Bend
Nat'l
Park

Presidio

Kerrville

Austin

New Braunfels

M

E

X

Chihuahua

I

C

O

Del Rio

Eagle
Pass

Uvalde

San Anto

Victoria

Rio Grande

Crystal City

Beeville

Parral

Nuevo Laredo

Laredo

Kingsville

Corp

SOUTHERN AND CENTRAL
UNITED STATES

Polyconic Projection

PADR
I.

McAllen

Harlinge

Brown

Scale of Miles

100   50   0   100   200

Matamoros

Capitals of Countries ⊛

State Capitals ◉

Ciudad Victoria

104 Longitude West of Greenwich

Chapter 4

Make a Plan

To use a map, start by finding where you are. Then, find where you want to go. Make a plan to get there.

Use the compass rose to move in the right direction. The scale shows how far you are going. Use the symbols to follow where you are on the map.

Fun Fact

Green triangles might mark trees and forests. Brown lines might show roads.

Make a Map

Create a map of your neighborhood. Be sure to give the map a title. Choose symbols and colors to stand for objects such as houses, parks, and roads. Make a key that shows what the different symbols and colors mean. Finally, write the names of important roads or buildings.

Reading a Map

Write your answers on a separate piece of paper.

1. Write a sentence explaining why people read maps.

2. What do you think is the hardest part of reading or using a map? Why?

3. What does a key show?
   - A. where north, south, east, and west are
   - B. how far apart areas on the map are
   - C. what the symbols and colors mean

4. How can people know if they are going in the right direction?
   - A. They use symbols on the map as a guide.
   - B. They read the title of the map.
   - C. They have to guess or ask a friend.

Answer key on page 24.

Glossary

compass rose
A symbol with four arrows showing north, south, east, and west on a map.

directions
Instructions for how to get from one place to another.

key
An area on a map that explains what the different symbols or colors mean.

overhead
Showing something from above.

scale
A map tool that shows how far apart places on a map are from one another in real life.

symbols
Marks or shapes that stand for something else.

title
The name of a book, map, or other work.

To Learn More

BOOKS

Brennan, Linda Crotta. *Maps: What You Need to Know.* North Mankato, MN: Capstone Press, 2018.

Nussbaum, Ben. *Making Maps.* Huntington Beach, CA: Teacher Created Materials, 2019.

NOTE TO EDUCATORS

Visit **www.focusreaders.com** to find lesson plans, activities, links, and other resources related to this title.

Index

Answer Key: 1. Answers will vary; **2.** Answers will vary; **3.** C; **4.** A